FEB 2 2 2010

Go-Kart Racing

The Thrill of Racing

LEE-ANNE T. SPALDING

Rourke
Publishing LLC
Vero Beach, Florida 32964

www.rourkepublishing.com

PHOTO CREDITS: ©The 359: page 5; © Honda Media/Dan Streck/LAT Photographic: page 7, 8, 9, 10, 12, 16 ; © Honda Media/ Paul Webb/ LAT Photographic: page 11; © Todd Taulman: page 13; © Honda Media/ LAT Photographic: page 18; © Honda Media/F. Peirce Williams/LAT Photographic: page 17, ; © Honda Media/Phillip Abbott/LAT Photographic: page 20, 21

Edited by Meg Greve

Cover design by Tara Raymo
Interior design by Teri Intzegian

Library of Congress Cataloging-in-Publication Data

Spalding, Lee-Anne T.

Go-kart racing / Lee-Anne T. Spalding.

p. cm. -- (The thrill of racing)

Includes index.

ISBN 978-1-60472-371-7

1. Karting--Juvenile literature. I. Title.

GV1029.5.S74 2009

796.7'6--dc22

2008011245

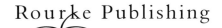

Rourke Publishing

www.rourkepublishing.com – rourke@rourkepublishing.com
Post Office Box 3328. Vero Beach. FL 32964

Table of Contents

History of Go-Kart Racing

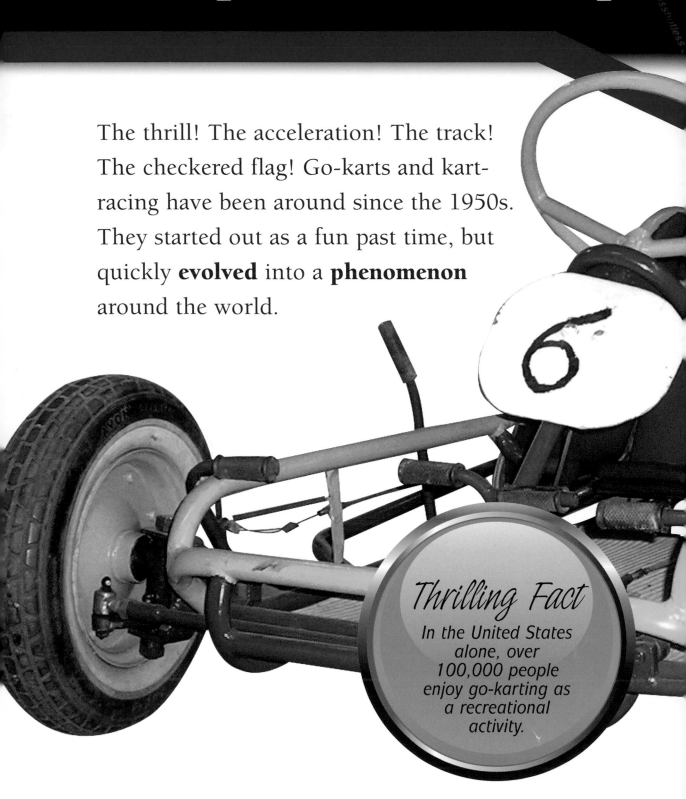

The thrill! The acceleration! The track! The checkered flag! Go-karts and kart-racing have been around since the 1950s. They started out as a fun past time, but quickly **evolved** into a **phenomenon** around the world.

Thrilling Fact

In the United States alone, over 100,000 people enjoy go-karting as a recreational activity.

An original go-kart from the 1950s.

Art Ingels

While working for Kurtis Kraft in southern California, Art Ingels built the very first go-kart in 1956.

A true go-kart has several basic parts: **chassis**, motor, transmission, steering wheel, seat, and four tires. Many have other **accessories** including: headlights, decals, roll cages, or aluminum rims.

A Safe Ride

Caged karts have a roll cage surrounding the driver. This roll cage protects the driver from injury while racing on dirt tracks.

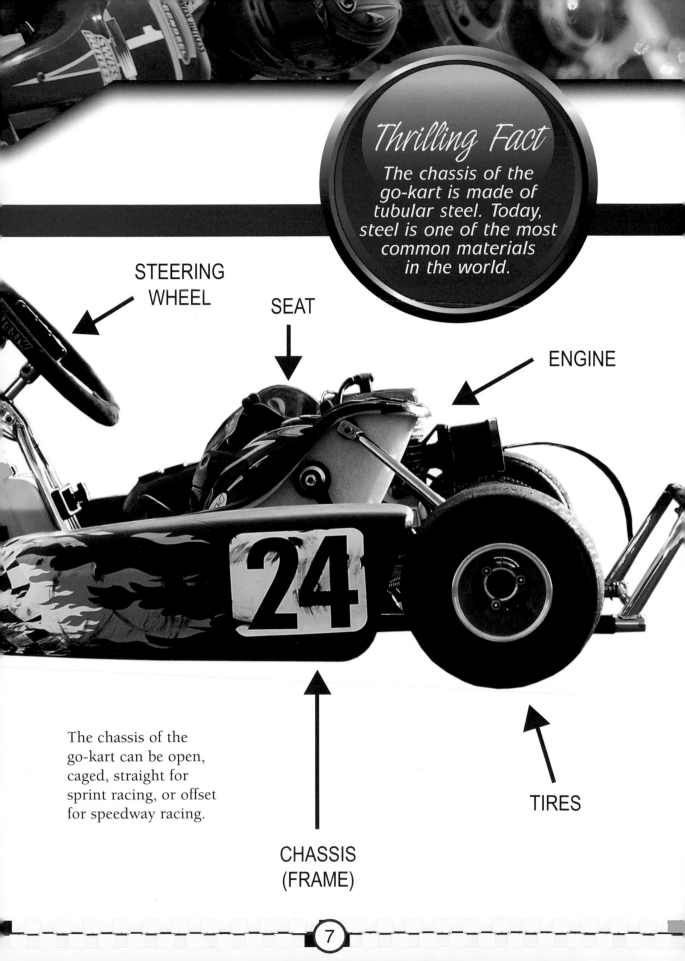

STEERING WHEEL

SEAT

ENGINE

Thrilling Fact

The chassis of the go-kart is made of tubular steel. Today, steel is one of the most common materials in the world.

The chassis of the go-kart can be open, caged, straight for sprint racing, or offset for speedway racing.

TIRES

CHASSIS (FRAME)

Kart Creations

Go-karts are built by many different companies all over the world. Well-known European **manufacturers** include Tony Kart, Top Kart, and Swiss Hutless. GT Race Karts, Shockwave Karting, and Trackmagic are all popular American companies.

You Asked...

How much does a go-kart weigh?

The average go-kart weighs between 165 and 175 pounds (75 to 79 kilograms) without a driver.

Kart Racing Rule Makers

The International Automobile Federation, known as FIA, regulates the sport of go-kart racing along with many other motorsports around the world. In the United States, the World Karting Association formed in 1971 to regulate and promote the sport of competitive kart racing.

Caution: Danger Zone

Go-karts look like fun rides but as with any moving vehicle, there is some danger involved. It is hard to believe, but a go-kart can travel at speeds up to 160 mph (257 km/h) which is as fast as many race cars travel on their tracks.

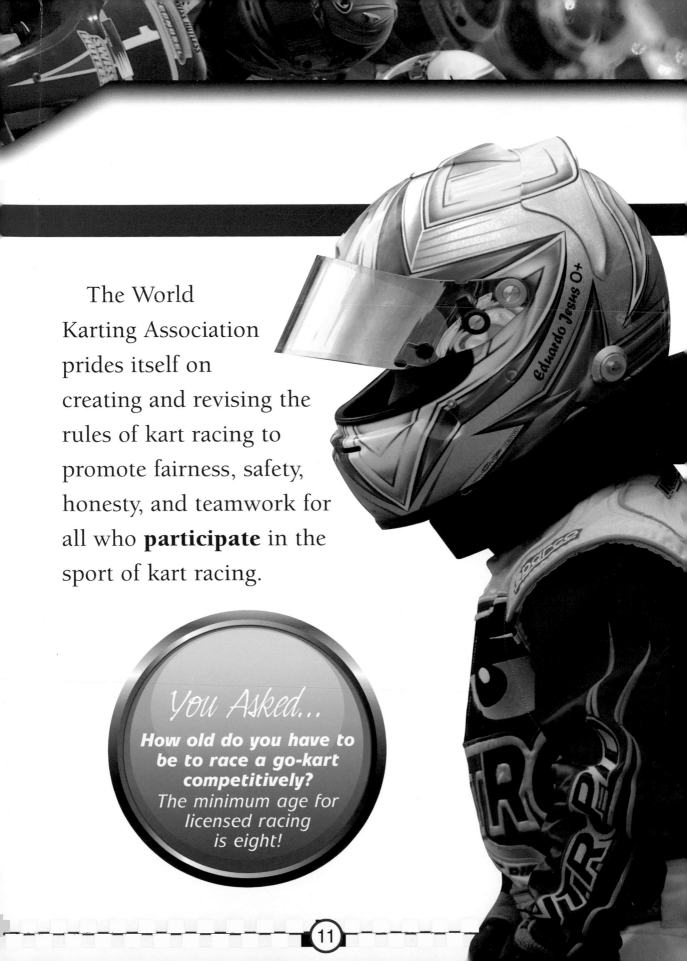

The World Karting Association prides itself on creating and revising the rules of kart racing to promote fairness, safety, honesty, and teamwork for all who **participate** in the sport of kart racing.

You Asked...

How old do you have to be to race a go-kart competitively?
The minimum age for licensed racing is eight!

Racing Formats

Go-karts typically race in three different formats. A sprint or short **duration** race, takes place on tracks that are usually one mile (1.6 kilometers) or less in length. These races last about 15 minutes.

On the other hand, endurance races are much longer. These races can last up to 24 hours. Finally, speedway races take place on asphalt or clay oval tracks. The tracks are usually one-quarter mile (402 meters) or less in length.

Start With Kart Racing

Kart racing can lead to racing professional Formula One or Indy cars. Formula One racing is the highest class of auto racing. Formula refers to the rules and requirements that all racers and race cars must meet.

Sarah Fisher

Sarah Fisher, a professional race car driver, got her start racing go-karts. Currently, she holds the record for being the youngest woman to ever race in the Indianapolis 500.

Many Formula One and NASCAR (National Association for Stock Car Racing) race car drivers got their start racing go-karts. Famous name drivers like Michael Schumacher, Tony Stewart, and Jeff Gordon all began their racing careers by racing on these small circuits.

Indy race cars or open wheel cars, race in popular events like the Indianapolis 500 at the Indianapolis Motor Speedway located in Speedway, Indiana. These cars differ from other race cars in that their wheels are located outside of the body of the car rather than underneath. The go-kart, having a similar body style, makes for great practice for future Indy car drivers.

Tony Stewart

Tony Stewart, born Anthony Wayne Stewart on May 20, 1971, is a current NASCAR driver. He began his racing career in go-karts. In 1987, he won the World Karting Championship at age 16. From there he raced Indy cars and stock cars. Tony made his NASCAR **debut** in 1996 and since then has won many events around the country.

Thrilling Fact

Indy cars race at speeds exceeding 220 mph (354 km/h).

Kart racing takes place all around the world. Organized events are available to children as young as five with competitive racing beginning at age eight. Beginners, called juniors, stay in groups for three years of racing, eventually making it to senior status at age 15 or 16.

Serious kart racers participate in **series** events year round. Some common series are Briggs & Stratton Speedway Dirt Series, Hortsman Gold Cup Series, and the Rage Kart Speedway Pavement Series. Many of these events take place on full-size tracks like the Daytona International Speedway in Daytona Beach, Florida and Lowe's Motor Speedway in Concord, North Carolina.

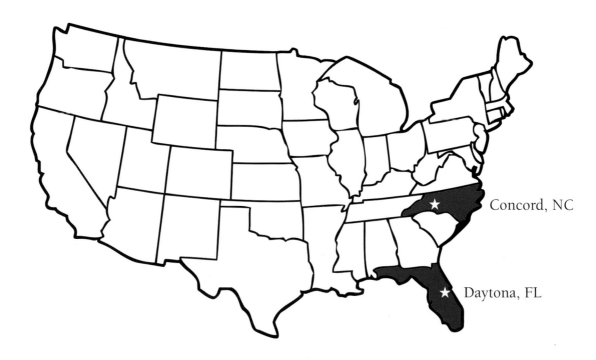

Concord, NC

Daytona, FL

Go-kart racing is less expensive than professional car racing. Basic models of new go-karts cost less than two thousand dollars while used models are even cheaper.

GO KART MODELS	PRICE
GK-01 (KTR-150A)	$1,688
GK-13B (250)	$2,528
GK-31 (KTR 1000)	$5,948
GK-34	$6,948

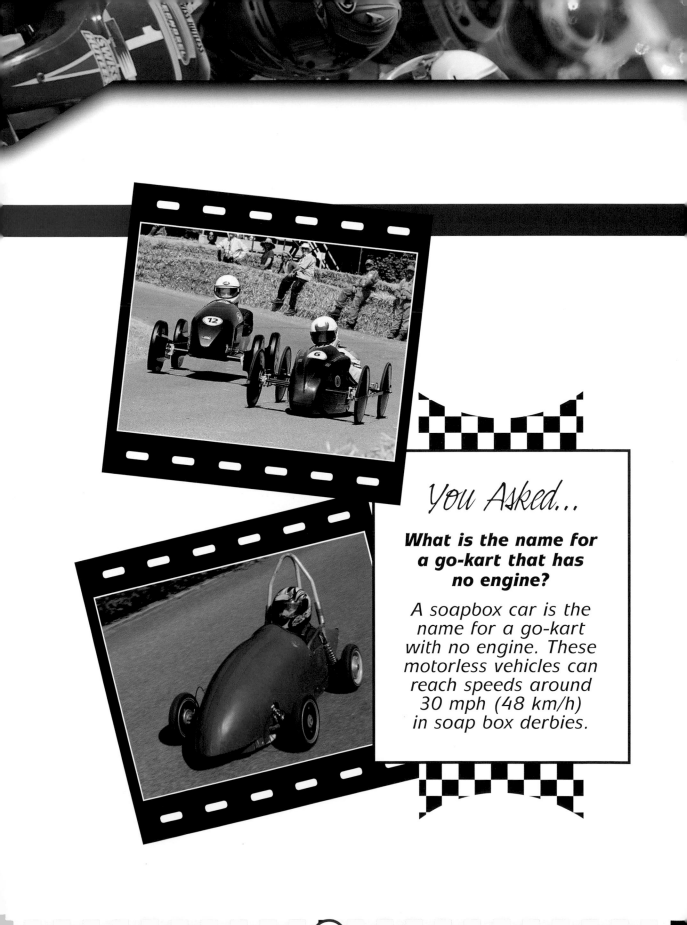

You Asked...

What is the name for a go-kart that has no engine?

A soapbox car is the name for a go-kart with no engine. These motorless vehicles can reach speeds around 30 mph (48 km/h) in soap box derbies.

Go-karts and kart racing have come a long way since the 1950s. Adults and children alike enjoy this sport, which has helped produce many great race car drivers. Whether riding just for fun or racing to win, go-karts are thrilling vehicles!

Glossary

accessories (ak-SESS-uh-rees): an extra part of something

chassis (CHASS-ee): the frame on which the body of a vehicle is built

debut (day-BYOO): a first public appearance

duration (du-RAY-shuhn): the period of time during which something lasts

evolved (i-VOLVD): to change slowly, sometimes over many years

formats (FOR-mats): the shape or style of something

manufacturers (man-yuh-FAK-chur-urs): to make something often with machines

participate (par-TISS-uh-pate): to join others in an activity or event

phenomenon (fe-NOM-uh-non): something very unusual or remarkable

series (SIHR-eez): a number of events that are linked in some way

Index

Websites to Visit

www.aboutkarting.com
www.go-carts-supreme.com
www.worldkarting.com

Further Reading

David, Jack. *Go-Kart Racing.* Bellwethe, 2008.

Doeden, Matt. *Shifter Karts: High-speed Go-karts.* Capstone Press, 2005.

Maddox, Jake and Suen, Anastasia. *Go-kart Rush (Impact Books. a Jake Maddox Sports Story).* Stone Arch Books, 2007.

About the Author

Lee-Anne Trimble Spalding is a former public school educator and is currently instructing preservice teachers at the University of Central Florida. She lives in Oviedo, Florida with her husband, Brett and two sons, Graham and Gavin.